TERRACES
& ROOF GARDENS
OF PARIS

Alexandra d'Arnoux
and Bruno de Laubadère

Photographs by
Deidi von Schaewen

Flammarion

Translated from the French by Lisa Davidson
Copy-editing: Sandra Raphael
Design: Caroline Chambeau
Typesetting: Julie Houis, À propos
Color separation: Sele Offset

Originally published as
Terrasses, un art de vivre en plein ciel
© 2001 Flammarion
English-language edition © 2002 Flammarion

ISBN: 2-0801-0624-4
N° d'édition: FA0624-01-XI
Dépôt légal: 03/2002
Printed and bound in Italy

Contents

Terraces with a view

Paris is a whole new experience from on high.
It no longer looks anything like the metropolis
we walk through every day. Nothing is quite
the same from the rooftops. Everyone has
experienced this at one time or another,
from the top of the Eiffel Tower, La Défense
Great Arch, or the Centre Georges Pompidou.
But a lucky few have their own private
terraces in apartments round the city which
have astonishing views. These rooftop terraces
open up new views of the French capital with
every changing season, as the light shifts from
dawn to dusk.

A view of the Eiffel Tower

Page 6: This terrace—a bucolic gem with a wild apple tree, hollyhocks, and a small sitting room of greenery—offers a spectacular view over Paris.

Below: View of the Grand Palais and the Petit Palais at dawn, with the skyscrapers of the Porte d'Italie in the background.

Opposite: The Eiffel Tower rises above this patch of greenery, complete with pear tree and bird's nest, growing amid a bed of hardy lavateras.

This apartment, with a spectacular view of the domes of the Grand Palais and the Petit Palais, is situated on the top floor of a building constructed in 1925 just a few steps away from the Champs-Élysées. It has two terraces: one facing southeast toward Avenue Matignon; the other southwest, with a view of the rooftops. Most of the major Paris monuments are visible from here, from the Eiffel Tower, of course, to the Madeleine, the church of Saint-Clotilde, the Assemblée Nationale, the tower of Saint-Sulpice, the Montagne Sainte-Geneviève, the Louvre, and, further away, the Tour Saint-Jacques and the Opéra. The dome of the Invalides can be seen from the living room, which leads to one of the terraces.

The owner of the apartment loves to walk around the terraces at dawn—the early-morning sky over Paris is often clear, and a few soft pink clouds lend the air a

Above left: A bird's-eye view of the pergola and white wisteria (Wisteria sinensis "Alba"), pruned as a shrub.

Above right: Potted plants line the wooden railings on the southern part of the terrace, which is well protected by trellis.

gentle feeling. It doesn't even matter if the weather changes later; the seemingly gray sky is far less uniform than you'd think, and has an infinite variety of nuances.

One of the terraces looks like a sitting room. It was created by the landscape designer Louis Benech, who put in a pergola covered in wisteria with long white flowers. A table and a few chairs, shaded by the pergola, provide a lovely place to eat in warm weather. Climbing roses and beds of choisyas add color and fragrance. Large potted evergreen box trees, pruned into spirals, structure the overall design by framing the doors leading from the apartment to the terrace.

The owner loves to prune these shrubs regularly to maintain their shape: "When you prune a box tree, it releases a wonderful strong scent. Pruning demands the eye of an illustrator. The pleasure lies in finding the ideal cut to create a curve that looks perfect to the eye. Yet you can't overdo it, as you'll cut too much and the pleasure of pruning soon turns into a disaster. When I have time, just after sunset, I prune and water the plants. There is not much street noise, but I hear lots of birds." When the terrace lamps are on and the monuments are illuminated, it's as if the inside and outside have melded into one, and you feel as though you're floating in space.

Above left: The garden furniture is slightly shaded by the white wisteria growing on the pergola. A climbing rose adds its own touch of white. In the foreground are choisyas.

Above right: Two evergreen box trees in topiary spirals frame a glass door.

A terrace balcony on the Left Bank

Above: A Nana, by Niki de Saint-Phalle, adds a colorful note to the upper terrace, in front of a flourishing border of Angustifolia lavender

Opposite: A bird's-eye view of the terrace balcony covered with red, pink, or white flowers, protected by a curtain of ivy. Two Nanas by Niki de Saint-Phalle dance on a low, sky-blue table.

Iranian artist Manijeh Torfeh has made her Paris home near the neighborhood of Saint-Germain-des-Prés. She is an interior designer and architect and used to work in various houses that belonged to the former Shah of Iran, including the famous palace on the Isle of Kish. Her apartment occupies two floors with a balcony outside the living room and, on the upper floor, a studio and office space with a glass roof. The view from the office is breathtaking: the street is far below, like the bottom of a ravine. A staircase at the back of the office leads to the terrace, which looks out over the rooftops.

The evening view is magical, especially when the monuments are illuminated by many spotlights. The bell-tower of Saint-Germain-des-Prés, the church of Saint-Sulpice, and, in the distance, the dome of the Académie de France are all visible. Just opposite is a series of handsome Haussmann buildings with domed roofs on the corners and balconies decorated with stone and marble columns.

Space is at a premium here, but the owner did not want to give up the pleasure of growing plants on her balcony. Ivy twines gracefully around the railing, transforming it into a low wall of vegetation, while a multitude of pots are filled with with seasonal flowers like geraniums and pansies in every shade of red and pink.

Manijeh Torfeh loves contemporary art and has many artists among her friends. She has placed several *Nanas* by Niki de Saint-Phalle among her flowers, creating a superb interplay of colors. One of these figures dances lightheartedly in the middle of a small round table, one of her own designs.

The owner created a small place to sit down on the upper terrace, with a few lavender borders, a couple of folding chairs, a low table (which she also designed) and, once again, a sculpture by Niki de Saint-Phalle to keep her company.

A panoramic view

This is, without any doubt, one of the most breath-taking views of Paris. The church of Saint-Sulpice is so close you want to reach out and touch it. The charming bell-tower of Saint-Germain-des-Prés stands on the left, followed by Notre-Dame, the dome of the Académie, and the Tour de Saint-Jacques. Montmartre rises up in the distance, illustrating another era and another theory of beauty. This terrace is at a perfect height; the foreground and background merge together seamlessly and the viewer can see the rooftops at eye level, with no sense of teetering over a vertiginous edge. And finally, the pattern formed by the terra-cotta chimney pots creates a series of miniature views like small paintings.

The owner loves architecture and designed this space herself. She feels that this apartment is like a real home, thanks to the terrace. The small staircase leading to the terrace looks like the kind of stairs which, in an old house, would lead up to the attic. In springtime, the chestnut trees on the square are covered with delicate light green leaves, which ripple in the breeze like gentle waves.

A certain disorder with an Italian air reigns over the terrace, forming part of its charm. The proximity of the church of Saint-Sulpice certainly contributes to the heavenly aura that seems to float in the air. The disorder is not, however, haphazard. It is a deliberate choice, an expression of freedom and insouciance. Vigorous plants reflect this refusal to be constrained. The roses —wild eglantine (brier rose) and "Iceberg"—mix well with pink and white hydrangeas, honeysuckle, and deep red, almost black geraniums.

The greenhouse, half-hidden in the vegetation, houses two surprising guests: a bird that never flies out, even when the door is left open, and a bust of Jean Racine,

Opposite: The branches of a Virginia creeper twine around the chimney pots; the leafy green creates a lovely contrast with the warm tones of the terra cotta. The church of Saint-Sulpice is visible on the right, while Notre-Dame stands dead center in the background.

Above: The dome of the Panthéon, visible beyond the church of Saint-Sulpice, towers over nearby buildings.

Following double page: This astonishing view stretches from the bell-tower of Saint-Germain-des-Prés to Montmartre in the distance.

Above: The church of Saint-Sulpice reflected in the bay window. The towers of Notre-Dame are visible in the distance on the left.

which is taken indoors for the winter like a delicate plant. The aluminum and glass greenhouse is not a particularly handsome structure, but placed here, it seems somewhat offbeat, a joking reference to a suburban garden shed. One day, it will probably disappear under the ivy and honeysuckle, shaded by the magnolia and maple which go on growing slowly.

The roofs nearby form a contrasting frame for this terrace. The clean straight lines of the building alternate with the oddly sloping shapes of the roofs—made of slate, concrete, zinc, or tiles. These roofs are topped with a forest of chimney pots, some small and slender,

This small greenhouse, nestling among flourishing greenery, houses a fine bust of Jean Racine.

others as massive as the chimneys of an imposing manor house in the country.

Seated on this rooftop terrace, looking out over the clouds, you will notice that the church bells do not sound quite the same up here as they do when you are standing down on the ground below. From the streets, the bells of Saint-Sulpice seem to be calling the streams of people to order, whereas from the terrace the ringing bells beckon the spirit into the wide open space up above.

Meditating in the open air

Above: The large, scented, white flowers of Magnolia grandiflora *stand out from the wall of plants surrounding the terrace. The Eiffel Tower rises in the background.*

Opposite: A deck chair, placed on aged teak decking, is an enticing spot to dream and meditate against the backdrop of the wide-open sky.

The creator of Léonard fabrics is a very busy man who understands the value of his scant leisure time. He loves his work and finds it eminently satisfying, but he returns happily to his terrace, where he feels entirely at home. The whole terrace is open to the sky, as it has only a low railing round it. Suddenly his time is his own: social constraints drop away and he can feel completely free.

From this terrace, which occupies a major section of the roof of a modern building near the Parc de La Muette, the details of everyday life seem far away indeed. The uninterrupted view stretches straight across the capital and you can enjoy the panorama as if it were a plan of the landmarks, with the Eiffel Tower acting as the needle of a compass in the dead center.

The library looks like a semaphore signal, with large bay windows facing the uncluttered, Zen-like terrace, which runs all around the apartment. The wooden deck, made of long planks arranged in a sort of irregular checkerboard pattern, is made of teak, which has aged into a lovely gray patina. The railing and the garden furniture are also painted in light but rather cool colors, forming a pleasant contrast with the various greens of the foliage—from the light green bamboo to the shiny, dark green of the magnolia leaves.

Given that the building is fairly high, the terrace is far above the hustle and bustle of the streets below. The delicate rustle of the bamboo leaves is the only sound to break the silence which reigns. A few magnolias (*Magnolia grandiflora*), with large white flowers and an intoxicating scent, add a gentle note of color to this delightful terrace garden which is an ideal location for meditating in the open air.

Terraces
in bloom

Is it possible to cultivate your own garden on
the rooftops of Paris? For some people, this
dream is an everyday reality. These privileged
owners of terraces satisfy their passion for
flowers in a world apart, protected by high
walls of shrubs and shaded by umbrella pines.
You can sometimes catch glimpses of these
hidden gardens from the street, high up on
buildings crowned with luxuriant vegetation
and occasional tall and splendid trees. Rooftop
gardeners toil away happily, far from the
noise and agitation of the streets below.

Olivia Putman's spray of flowers

Page 22: A collection of odd pots and containers under a lovely Clematis montana. *A clump of* Anthemis *in the foreground adds a bright touch to this half-shaded corner.*

Above: This flower-filled bed is designed like a small mixed garden. Umbellifers and lavenders grow alongside royal lilies.

Opposite: A bird's-eye view of the summer dining room. This section of the terrace is lined with large yellow euphorbias and mauve-colored wallflowers on the left; in the center is the white Convolvulus cneorum. *Climbing roses and jasmine cover the walls.*

Olivia Putman's terrace is a gigantic bouquet of flowers. A landscape designer and enthusiastic botanist, she uses her expertise to combine colors and keep her garden in bloom all year round. She has specialized in the design of terraces for several years, and her projects are distinguished by their unique charm and perfect harmony. The gardens are always in keeping with the spirit of each individual place. Designing a terrace garden is a fascinating challenge. There are always —or almost always—serious constraints: the space available is often too narrow or poorly laid out; elements of the environment may need to be accentuated or, on the contrary, hidden; and there may be a microclimate, which is not always beneficial to the plants (too much wind, and not enough or too much sun). For Olivia Putman, these challenges are stimulating. She experiments with new ideas on her own terrace. This is where she dreams up and tests new combinations of plant and checks whether they can survive in the Paris climate.

When she moved to the 16th *arrondissement*, the large terrace had only a few hastily planted tubs. She started by creating large flowerbeds around the edge of the terrace and keeping an open space in the center, where she placed a table and chairs. A second narrow terrace runs the length of the apartment; it is edged with trellis covered with *Trachelospermum jasminoides* and golden hops.

Contrary to popular belief, nature is never fully dormant, and a good gardener selects plants in order to have flowers in bloom all year round—as this terrace does, with color throughout the seasons. For the colder months she chose winter jasmine, *Jasminum nudiflorum*, which is covered with small yellow flowers from January (though the flowers do not have any scent). Other plants on her terrace also bloom in winter: camellias (*Camellia sasanqua*), which flower throughout

This small sitting area is surrounded by plants.
A few deck chairs provide inviting places
to sit in the cool shade. A metal sphere,
in the bed to the left near a round boxwood,
perpetuates an Austrian tradition
of paying tribute to the fertility of nature.

the autumn into early winter; greenish hellebores (*Helleborus orientalis*) or Christmas roses (*H. niger*), with delicate pinkish-white flowers that stand out against deeply divided leaves; *Stachyurus praecox*, a shrub covered in late autumn with long buds, which form clusters of pale green flowers in February; and daphnes (*Daphne odora*), with wonderfully fragrant white flowers.

Spring ushers in an explosion of color: pale yellow lilies set off deep blue *Iris sibirica* and miniature lilac (*Syringa meyeri* "Palibin"), which scents the Paris air early in the season. Other sweet-smelling plants include the choisyas, which are marvelous small orange-scented trees from

The wisteria-covered trellis protects the small garden area from the wind and keeps it cool.

Mexico, and *Viburnum plicatum* "Watanabe", with creamy-white flowers in repeated waves during its season.

Roses and clematis climb the walls, transforming them into giant bouquets. *Rosa chinesis* "Mutabilis" is one of Olivia Putman's special favorites. The flowers are first a dusty yellow color and turn dark pink as they fade. There are several kinds of clematis on the terrace; one of the most remarkable is *Clematis montana* "Rubens", with long-lasting, slightly fragrant, pale or dark pink flowers. She also has the double-flowered clematis "Vyvyan Pennell" and *Clematis armandii*, which are both evergreen.

Above left: The long stems of Iris sibirica are topped with superb, velvety purple flowers.

Above right: Lavandula stoechas, with mauve-colored tufts of flowers, looks like a hat stuck with feathers.

Olivia Putman also planted euphorbias; she loves the delicate indented bluish-gray leaves and the strange yellow-green blossoms that appear in the spring and often last through early summer.

During the summer, the large flowerbeds are dominated by yellow euphorbia flowers. Then they move onto a splendid range of colors with summer wallflowers and lavender, whose gray-green leaves contrast with the deeper green in the beds nearby. *Convolvulus cneorum* occupies the heart of the beds; this is a magnificent shrub with silky, silver leaves, covered all summer with pearly pink flowers, which turn white as they age.

They are as charming as some of the wild flowers related to them, for example, bindweed or morning glory.

"I set up a large teak bench on my terrace," says Olivia Putman, "a simple copy of an English park bench, but the advantage of this wood is that it takes on a gray patina over time—so that as the years pass, it matches the rest of the garden even better. I spend long hours on it, resting and reading. A bronze with a lovely patina by the sculptor Rheinoud keeps me company, as do the birds, which appreciate my open-air garden. The terrace faces east, toward the rising sun, and is marvelous in the morning."

Above left: A "President" clematis. Olivia Putman chose a harmonious range of colors for her clematis, ranging from blue to mauve and white.

Above right: The beautiful elongated blossoms of the unusual Phlox maculata.

Odd pots

The owner of this terrace feels that growing flowers in pots offers total freedom: the freedom to plant whichever flowers she wants, to alter combinations of colors as she sees fit, and to grow them in any possible kind of container (the more unusual the better)—not to mention the freedom to toss out plants that are no longer in bloom or that she no longer likes. She considers freedom to be an essential element of gardening. This is, in fact, one of the reasons she loves her terrace so much. "Here, away from everyone, we can rediscover who we really are. We are free to do what we like, to spend our time as we please."

The terrace is decorated with all kinds of odds and ends: a pier glass picked up from a friend who deals in antiques, Nicole Alterao; a few pieces of stained glass; a collection of bottles; and an assortment of sculptures from Malaysia.

The variety of containers is surprising: a large shell is filled with helxine (*Soleirolia soleirolii*), looking exactly like a pond covered with algae; a terra-cotta basin has a large clump of marguerites; and a zinc container overflows with lavender.

Near the bench are a few almond trees, which are covered with clouds of pink buds in late March. The Mediterranean plants thrive in pots and are placed together: thyme, rosemary, and hybrid lavender are combined with "butterfly" French lavender (*Lavandula stoechas*), which produces its odd-looking flowers in late April. A large Virginia creeper climbs up the walls that enclose the terrace. In the fall, its leaves are transformed into an immense tapestry of varying shades of red, a background for many different species of potted chrysanthemums. The dark, velvety clematis "Red Cardinal" is particularly hardy: it has been on the terrace for thirty years and is a particular favorite.

Above: Helxine, planted in a large white shell and placed under a Chamaecyparis hedge, evokes dormant water covered with algae.

Opposite: A basket of blooming Lavandula stoechas stands in front of a row of almond trees.

Following double page: A large pier glass, placed near the bay window in the light-filled veranda, creates an illusion of depth. A Ficus lirata is reflected in the mirror.

A flower-filled balcony

Above: A bouquet of pink nasturtiums.

Opposite: A spectacular display of flowering plants, including dahlias, cosmos, petunias, campanulas, geraniums, fuchsias, and begonias.

Mohanjeet is Indian and loves Paris, where she has been living for many years. She runs an art gallery, where she exhibits works by contemporary Indian artists. She lives in the Montparnasse neighborhood, on the top floor of a Haussmann building. An avid gardener, she has transformed her balcony into a great basket of flowers. Her selection of plants displays a marked preference for those with pure colors. She chooses warm shades—reds, yellows, and oranges—along with softer colors—pinks and whites. The contrasting colors create a lovely effect that looks something like a fine embroidery or tapestry.

This terrace has many types of flowers: some look wild, like the foxgloves, with long spikes of helmet-shaped purple flowers; others, like linaria (toadflax) and snapdragons, flourish on the old walls. She has more traditional balcony plants, such as brightly colored hydrangeas, tuberous begonias, and geraniums (that is, pelargoniums), as well as flowers more often found in meadows than in the city. These include campanulas, sunflowers, and wild daffodils, along with low-maintenance plants, such as pansies and petunias, which have charming colors. There are exotic flowers, such as hibiscus and nasturtiums; and simpler flowers, like cosmos and humble cornflowers, which add a cheery note; and finally, flowers with more complicated shapes, such as chrysanthemums or large yellow and black dahlias.

Mohanjeet's exuberant and constantly blooming balcony is a joyful patch of color that seems to link two ancient cultures.

A colorful terrace

The terrace of this house, which belongs to the creator of Siki de Somalie jewelry, is a haven of peace and happiness. Nestled in a private street in the 16th *arrondissement*, it offers a secret retreat from the noise and bustle of the city. The colorful exuberance of the plants is an unequaled source of visual pleasure.

When you first enter this terrace, the most striking impression is the spectacular brightness of the colors: the flowerbeds are filled with pink, red, violet, orange, yellow, and white flowers. Many scented plants also grow here. The owner has a particular fondness for jasmines, gardenias, choisyas, hyacinths, sweet williams, and fragrant pelargoniums. Roses bloom everywhere, especially the lovely ivory-colored "Thérèse de Lisieux" and the small, climbing "Aloha" rose (a deep pink, repeat-flowering rose, the name of which is a greeting from Hawaii).

Below left: A bouquet of "Anita Pereire" roses.

Below right: An azalea with red flowers.

Opposite: The terrace viewed from the top floor of the apartment. The white flowers of the clematis and the marguerites stand out against a background of diverse green foliage.

The owner loves flower arranging and creates spectacular bouquets that combine sophisticated flowers with other, wilder blooms. She therefore has large clumps of marguerites scattered throughout the beds. She also takes care to cultivate other contrasts, such as fragile poppies, with delicate silky petals, alongside lovely winter-blooming hellebores and the strongly sculptural acanthus, which has deely divided leaves and imposing spikes of flowers.

She loves the profusion of plants, which gives a baroque look to her terrace. This is one of the reasons she chooses species that flower generously, for example, climbing roses with a multitude of flowers. Another favorite is *Clematis montana*, whose long branches, covered with white star-shaped flowers, reach across the veranda. The small flowers of some fuchsias offer a calm respite, at least until the bougainvillea, honeysuckle, and passionflowers, not to mention many hundreds of cyclamen, create a riotous burst of color. The atmosphere of this small patch of nature in the very heart of the city can be summed up in a single word: opulence.

The Victorian veranda, complete with fluted columns, is painted dark blue, a color that sets off the white clematis flowers that cover most of it. It has been transformed into a comfortable sitting room, which leads to the planted terrace. The lemon tree is often inside, not so much because it cannot withstand the cold—the temperatures in Paris are rarely that low—, but so that the owner can fully enjoy its delicate scent inside the apartment. The small mandarin orange trees are also brought inside every so often. They may not have any scent, but their wonderfully decorative leaves more than make up for this.

This profusion of colors makes the terrace a source of delight during the day. In good weather, when it's possible to eat outdoors at night, it's as peaceful as being in the countryside. The lamps create a soft, intimate glow over the table, fostering late-night conversation.

Above: The veranda is covered with white Clematis montana.

Below: A metal garden chair, surrounded by a pot of arum lilies and small mandarin orange trees.

Opposite: Large marguerites, pansies, and poppies.

A rose garden

This terrace with a thousand flowers has a view of the Bois de Boulogne, which seems to stretch as far as the horizon. Yet the owners had to create a hedge of *Chamaecyparis* on one side to provide a windbreak for other plants. They started by planting a cedar, with the idea of repeating one of the elements from the nearby forest. But the tree grew so tall that it had to be removed. The terrace surrounding the apartment is designed like a real garden, with a lawn and a path made of large, flat, stepping stones. There are trees—blue or green pines and "Floribunda" magnolias—and quantities of flowers: varieties of red and white camellias that flower for a long time, wild quince trees (japonica), and masses of rhododendrons and azaleas. The real treasure of this terrace is the magnificent collection of roses, including red roses, tea roses, white roses (such as "Iceberg"), and yellow roses, among them the incomparable "Mermaid."

Below: A large bed of "Catherine Deneuve" roses.

Opposite: The terrace surrounding the apartment is enclosed by a hedge of Chamaecyparis. *Slabs of stone form a pathway through the lawn, which is lined with a lovely collection of rose bushes.*

Hollyhock terrace

"We had a balcony and dreamed of creating a terrace filled with flowers," say the owners. "After some remodeling, we were able to fulfill our dream. The apartment lost a few square meters inside, but gained a larger balcony and more light." Once large amounts of soil had been brought in, the balcony was transformed into a magnificently colorful and intimate garden, complete with an automatic watering system.

Tall yew trees form a backdrop to the profusion in the beds. Hyacinths, tulips, and crocuses are the first to appear as winter moves on to its close. Next to flower are the annuals and climbing plants. Clematis thrives here, and with nearly a dozen varieties ranging in color from blue to white, there is always at least one in bloom throughout the spring and summer months. *Clematis montana* is the first to flower. They grow alongside honeysuckle, repeat-flowering roses, and lupins, which have a delicate, slightly peppery fragrance. A few pink tree peonies then make a sumptuous, though short-lived, appearance. The scented lilies and the delphiniums bloom, and are gradually replaced by hollyhocks, which thrive so well here.

Flowering shrubs with white, red, and pink colors (large shrub roses, rhododendrons, azaleas, and hydrangeas) were used to create an impression of height in the flowerbeds. A few marguerites add a note of simplicity and spontaneity.

The owners decided to add fruit trees to their lovely mixture of shrubs and flowers, just like a country garden. These include an apple tree and a grafted plum tree, which produces delicious nectarines. A vine winds up and around a pergola. Nearby, a lemon tree and an olive tree offer a touch of the south of France. Robins and blackbirds often fly over from the nearby garden of the Rodin Museum for a visit.

Above: This pretty garden table, standing in the midst of the plants, waits for guests.

Opposite: This luxuriant garden looks as though it was brought straight from the south of France. The overgrown garden includes Clematis montana, *along with hollyhocks and tobacco flowers (in the foreground).*

A garden under glass

Above: A magnificent acanthus in full bloom.

*Opposite: A view overlooking a large bed
of eglantines (wild or dog roses).*

*Page 46: Pots of rhododendrons and
pansies stand in front of the greenhouse.*

Page 47: Inside, an abundance of pots and flowers.

This duplex apartment features two linked terraces. The smaller of the two extends from the bedrooms. The larger one, which is on the lower level, has a large flowerbed full of climbing roses. In the background, towering over the nearby buildings, is a church dome that gives the view something of an Italian air. The eglantine roses, nearly all wild ones, bloom profusely. The clusters of white flowers stand out magnificently against the dark green foliage. The owner, an American living in Paris, covered the edge of her terrace with trellis on which she grows a relatively uncommon species of hydrangea, *Hydrangea petiolaris.* It has light green leaves, which are small and rounded, and is covered with ravishing white flowers that have a scent like honey. Clematis and Virginia creeper grow alongside this hydrangea, creating a sumptuous cover for the trellis and walls.

Large flowerpots and containers, with boxwood clipped into balls and lavender bushes, are placed all over the terraces. Some of the lavenders have also been pruned, while others are left to grow freely. A *Hydrangea quercifolia* also grows in a pot; it has panicles of ivory-colored flowers pricked with pink centers. The large, toothed leaves resemble the foliage of some large American oaks, which turns a deep red in the autumn. Other surprising plants fill up the flowerbed. These include acanthus, which flourishes near the tree peonies and the azaleas. A few potted annuals—white pansies and sweet peas—contribute even more color to this profusion, while several "Iceberg" roses add an iridescent white in the fall.

Finally, the greenhouse looks like a workshop with bird cages and boxes filled with dormant bulbs and plant cuttings. Nearby is the household's favorite plant: an olive tree which produces enough fruit each year to give a liter of oil.

Robinson Crusoe in Paris

Some terraces look like an open-air artist's studio, a creative jumble of surprises. They are as much fun to explore as an attic, with the same feeling of freedom as being out in a meadow, the same sense of peace as in the desert. There's a wonderful sense of well-being as the wind blows and the sun shines, not to mention the sounds of silence. The Robinson Crusoes of Paris have the souls of explorers, art collectors, and antique dealers—and often, green thumbs as well. All of them enjoy the daily pleasure of having a space where they can let their imaginations run free.

Charming chaos

Page 48: A small cabin, nestling among wild grasses in the heart of Paris.

Below: An extraordinary wealth of vegetation covers the terrace rooftops.

Opposite: A staircase and door are concealed by bamboo and the foliage of Hydrangea petiolaris. *The house has practically disappeared under the greenery.*

For renowned landscape designer Camille Muller, the art of gardening means knowing how to take time. Nature likes to live at its own pace, and should never be pushed to do otherwise. In the gardens he designs, the plants all look as if they grow exactly as they please. In the words of Gilles Clément, Muller's professor at the Lille School of Landscape Architecture, they form "a lovely tangle" in which curves and masses are more important than geometric forms. Once Muller, a farmer's son, came to Paris, he found the urban environment too inhuman. He immediately looked for a space to live where he could create a refuge, like "a cabin lost in the woods." Indeed, the forest is an environment he has known since childhood: "My grandmother sent me out to gather blackberries, branches of spindle trees, and wild roses. I planted them on the rooftops in my village in Alsace. They would bloom for Mother's Day."

In Paris, Camille finally found his "cabin," a covered courtyard with a patio alongside a house. He transformed the roof into a terrace with a marvelous hanging garden. He feels at home here, perched on the roof as if he were living on an island, surrounded by plants with only the sky overhead. Everything thrives here; many of the plants were rescued and brought to this haven for a second chance. Surrounded by walls, the terrace garden is overgrown with plants: vines, ivy, honeysuckle, and roses, which have the advantage of being almost evergreen.

Camille Muller uses every inch of his terrace, including many slopes of the roof, as supports for pots and larger containers. In an area in which the former occupants used to store wood, he designed a small corner terrace in which he placed a thornless Bohemian olive tree. Flowers are everywhere: wild balsams, wallflowers, old roses, including a superb "Ronsard," and scented geraniums. There are also some lovely shrubs with white flowers (*Sorbaria*); an *Akebia*, with red flowers in the spring; and oleasters (*Elaeagnus angustifolia* and *E. commutata*) have sweet-smelling flowers. And if all this were not enough, there's also an enormous pot of boxwood alongside a large cypress, an espaliered apple tree, a Virgina creeper (*Parthenocissus quinquefolia*), and a few tomato plants.

"Here, more than anywhere else, I let disorder reign, because this is my home," admits Camille Muller with a smile. "I kept a privet that started here by accident, probably brought in by a bird. I love the scent of its flowers." Everything grows in containers, fed by an automatic watering system and just a single type of fertilizer, bonemeal, because the water drains out of the containers into a basin with a few goldfish. "One of my greatest joys here are the birds that come to see me every night: blackbirds, starlings… Sometimes there are even bats. I once conducted an experiment: I planted a Portuguese cabbage to see whether its usual companion, *Pieris*, would find it in the middle of Paris. Well, one day I looked up and saw this white butterfly flitting around my cabbage!"

Above: A lovely bird-house on the wall.

Below: An Italian glass lamp, suspended from a cypress tree, illuminates the staircase.

Opposite: This magnificent terrace looks like a rustic country garden.

The gardener's tool shed

Maintaining a vegetable garden is no small matter: it needs lots of time and good soil. It may be a crazy idea to create this type of garden on a rooftop terrace, but keep in mind the pleasure of inspecting the "grounds" every day, fighting off unwelcome slugs, digging and hoeing with pint-sized tools and, above all, savoring your own vegetables.

This house, designed in the 1930s as an artist's studio by Auguste Perret, has two terraces. The first, which has a view over the gardens, is designed as a peaceful spot; it has an austere charm, punctuated by lines of pruned boxwood. The second, on the roof of the house, is the pride and joy of the owner, a journalist who specializes in gardening. She likes to get her hands dirty, take cuttings, and watch plants grow, so she did not hesitate to transform her 90-square-meter terrace into a flower-filled vegetable garden.

The walls surrounding the terrace are covered with ivy and honeysuckle. A row of large terra-cotta pots, planted with cherry trees and ivy trained into spherical shapes, accompany a small willow, whose twisted trunk is supported by one of the walls. Gravel paths make it easy to walk between the four large wooden frames, filled with vegetables and flowers. A covered "Lou Fagotin" bench offers a shady place to rest, off to one side of the garden.

One of the frames is entirely filled with herbs; it's a miniature physic garden, with various species of mint, common thyme, lemon thyme, parsley, and basil. A beautiful floribunda rose, "Fée des Neiges," with large, pure white flowers, grows right next to the frame, combining its subtle fragrance with the strong scents of the herbs. The other frames contain tightly spaced rows of vegetables: radishes, lettuce, and other salad greens, including romaine, endive, oak-leaf

Above: Glass bells designed by Cléophée de Turkheim stand in front of large terra-cotta pots planted with cherry trees.

Opposite: A gravel path, a low wall at the back, and a tiled rooftop create the impression of a real country garden. (In the foreground): Right, Hydrangea quercifolia, and left, a bed planted with ornamental alliums.

lettuce, green and red beans, and even tiny fragrant wild strawberries.

The terrace is not very big, so a few medium-sized plants provide an agreeable structure for the space. The magnificent foliage of angelicas and acanthus, mixed with tall ornamental grasses, counterbalances the strict geometry of the vegetable frames. There are also large shrubs of broad-leafed *Hydrangea quercifolia* and rustic white Japanese anemones, which go well with the white buddleia.

A bench, a few stools, and red Chinese chairs are placed around a potting table stacked with labels, shears, and pots of all sizes. In the spring, daffodils, jonquils, narcissi, and tulips fill a large part of the frames. In the autumn, asters and the rounded leaves of a *Vitis coignetiae* produce a riot of colors.

Below left: At the end of the season, rose hips grow if the flowers are not cut; they provide a decorative touch throughout the winter.

Below right: A series of pots wait for new plants.

Opposite: Two wooden frames contain vegetables and herbs. (In the foreground): Ornamental grasses and a clump of Gunnera.

Ivy and honeysuckle

Above: An Indian colored glass lamp, suspended from a pergola covered with honeysuckle.

Opposite: At night, several lamps create a poetic setting under the pergola covered with ivy, jasmine, honeysuckle, and golden hops.

There was once no terrace on the top floor of this Haussmann-style building in Paris's 7th *arrondissement*; there was just the slope of a small roof, which was totally useless to the resident. The owner asked architect Bernard Wautier Wursmer to redesign the area; he suggested removing the roof and replacing it with a long narrow terrace. Its charm comes from the quality of the materials used. The ground was covered with teak floorboards; the strong trellis was also made of wood that ages well, acquiring a patina as it does so. Ivy and honeysuckle cover the trellis entirely, along with a lovely white wisteria, fragrant jasmine, and hops.

The owner is an avid traveler and brought back from India old lamps made of deep green and blue glass. He suspended them from the trellis overhanging the plants. When they're lit up at night, they project a mysterious, gentle light, which creates an exotic atmosphere in the heart of the city. The four windows leading to the terrace are also illuminated by small lamps.

"What I like here," confides the owner, "is the unaffected style, something like a small mixed garden. In the pots lining the walls I planted birthwort, which has odd-shaped flowers; an *Actinidia*, a shrub originally from China which has pretty white flowers in June; and kiwifruit, passionflowers, and a few hydrangeas—all in shades of white for a harmonious color scheme."

The terrace, protected by the trellis, offers a charming picture of well-ordered chaos; it has a somewhat abandoned although elegant look about it, which is actually the result of meticulous care and strict maintenance. The owner often eats outside in this intimate atmosphere. In the mornings, the birds take over.

Other worlds

This terrace, located on the roof of a 1930s building in Neuilly, belongs to an avid gardener; several years ago, she decided to replace the existing tennis court with a hanging garden. She has traveled extensively in Asia and therefore wanted her garden to have a sense of far-off places and a feeing of the Orient. "One day," she says, "when I was visiting the Jardin des Plantes, I discovered some magnificent ornamental grasses, and at the same time, a gardener who was more than willing to help me choose which plants to place on my terrace. I love gardens, but because flowers are hard to grow in these high places, bamboo and grasses seemed an obvious choice. I was probably one of the first to introduce ornamental grasses to terraces. I bought them in England."

She started by constructing a willow house for her small son, along with a large sandbox. The following spring, however, the willow had taken root in the damp sand and the house started to sprout leaves. No matter how much she cut the shoots, they continued to thrive. The small boy has since grown up, and the house has become more of a tree, a willow with long, supple, yellow branches.

The terrace is protected by a windbreak, created by a hedge of heather, ferns, and gorse, topped with stalks of giant bamboo which hold them in place and create a Japanese-style wall. Kiftsgate roses, honeysuckle, and vines partially cover this enclosure.

Plant containers constructed and arranged in geometric patterns hold other bamboos and ornamental grasses: two varieties of reeds from Provence, *Arundo donax,* including the spectacular "Variegata," along with *Miscanthus sinensis*, pampas grass, four varieties of papyrus, including *Cyperus papyrus* itself, and horsetails. Everything thrives as if in a hot humid climate, thanks to the automatic watering system.

Above: The eccentric beauty of a Salix matsudana *"Tortuosa" or corkscrew willow, near the cabin.*

Opposite: A bamboo irrigation system under the leaves of a weeping birch keeps the soil cool and damp enough to grow ornamental grasses.

Following double page: An eclectic collection of stones and objects, placed on the tiles surrounding the flowerbeds, sets off the potted plants, which include a hazel tree.

Above left: The gray stones and pieces of aged wood set off the light greens of Eriophorum angustifolium, *irises, and* Ophiopogon japonicum.

Above right: The smooth texture of the stones and small rock garden contrast with the variety of leaves of the potted plants.

There is, of course, a frame for herbs, with fennel, Chinese garlic, lemon balm, and a few Japanese herbs, including myoga (which resembles ginger) and mitsuba (which is like Japanese watercress). There is also a frame reserved for vegetables, including miniature carrots. These are not the only crops, however: every year, the olive tree produces olives, a dwarf hazel produces nuts, vines give six kilograms (fifteen pounds) of grapes, and as for the cherry tree, the results depend entirely on what the birds leave behind.

Among the rare flowers growing in this terrace is the chocolate cosmos, which came from Great Britain.

Another surprise is the beautiful collection of hollies: there are many varieties with small leaves or variegated yellow foliage.

The owner has arranged lots of objects around the growing frames as offerings to nature: stones, stumps, gravel, and shells. She and her husband returned from the Sologne region with a stump that had to be hauled up in a sheet, because the elevator doesn't reach this top floor.

Above left: The foliage of Imperata cylindrica *"Rubra," Geranium "Johnson's Blue," and Kilmarnock willow forms a harmony of colors.*

Above right: A short poem written in white on a blackboard pays tribute to the bamboo Pseudosasa japonica.

Beyond the birch trees

The monotony of the street below is instantly forgotten once you set foot in this small paradise. The terrace is arranged on three levels and is protected on three sides by a wall of birch trees brought back from a forest. They grow marvelously well in jerrycans cut in half. The owners wanted to create a simple and peaceful world apart, sheltered from the noise of the city. In the summer, they eat and often even sleep on the terrace. Everything they need is here, from candles to tables and mosquito nets.

Plants flower all through the seasons. Lilacs appear in the spring, followed soon after by a colorful profusion of irises, while hydrangeas bloom all summer long. Different varieties of geraniums (pelargoniums) add bright colors from April to December. They are planted alongside sweet peas, *Cornus, Viburnum,* laurels, and choisyas (small fragrant orange-scented shrubs from Mexico).

Below: A large room leading to the wall of young birch trees surrounding the terrace is used as a greenhouse for plants like hydrangeas, petunias, and pelargoniums, which can't survive outdoors.

Opposite: A net stretched on the wall as a support for climbing plants creates an unusual effect.

Astonishing terraces

A terrace in the sky of Paris is, by definition, a special site, far removed from the urban reality of the city below. It is often surprising—possibly because it has no specific function. Everything is possible here; there are no limits to what the imagination can conjure up: pools to swim in among the clouds or rooftop vegetable gardens that look like Surrealist work. These astonishing terraces are like doorways to a dream world.

Andrée Putman's terrace

Andrée Putman loves the *joie de vivre* and freedom of her terrace, both of which are important to her creativity. She has given form to her vision in this large sheltered space, surrounded by rooftops and walls covered with ivy and honeysuckle. It is a coherent scheme that incorporates the dynamic movement of plants and her contemporary sense of design.

Indeed, many designers are represented on Andrée Putman's terrace: the armchairs are by Mallet-Stevens and the rock-work bench is the work of antique dealer Comoglio. It is painted an ashy gray-blue, the same color as her childhood home, the same delicate color of cigarette smoke. A weathervane by the artist Rolland Roure stands out against the blue sky; it looks like a kite, with a red face painted on one side, a blue face on the other.

The furniture is not the only creative element. There are other, humbler objects, like a large pot filled with

Page 68: A large climbing rose, "Landora," with yellow flowers, frames the window in the trellis overlooking the Eiffel Tower.

Below: The kitchen is below ground level and is constructed like a greenhouse. The work surface is therefore at the same level as the terrace.

Opposite: In the foreground to the right is an armchair designed by Mallet-Stevens, next to an acanthus planted in a large pot inlaid with pieces of a mirror, Gaudi-style.

Above: An Austrian sphere, half-hidden among the leaves, is reputed to bring good luck; part of the terrace is reflected on its surface.

Below: A weathervane designed by Rolland Roure.

Opposite: A beautiful bench from Comoglio, with an arabesque-style back, stands near the Mallet-Stevens armchairs.

acanthus, which is both a rustic and a refined flower. The pot is actually a barrel that has been coated with cement in which fragments of colored glass have been placed—a reference to the inlays used by the Spanish architect Gaudi, although northerners, too, apparently like to make this kind of pot; miners used to make them, perhaps to brighten up the monotony of their daily lives.

Even though Andrée Putman has a very busy social life, she is above all an artist and needs to be alone from time to time to reflect and to dream. What she likes above all, in these moments of freedom, is to commune with nature—or at least with this small patch of nature that she has made her own.

You can hear the wind on this terrace, as well as buzzing insects and the birds that return noisily at night to their nests hidden in the ivy.

She also spends a lot of time in her greenhouse. From the outside it looks like a real garden greenhouse, but in reality it is Andrée Putman's second secret garden: her kitchen, with a glass roof open to the sky, a large table, and bistro chairs. "I love to cook, it's almost the same as taking care of plants. Just as nature can help you become more centered, when you cook a meal, you feel more in tune with yourself. Here, I feel as though I'm on the deck of a ship."

She visits her terrace early in the morning as she likes to see the fresh colors of the dawn, and the rapidity with which the sun comes up and the light changes. She never grows tired of experiencing the ever-changing seasons or watching the very first flowers bloom in the springtime.

Happiness is something that is best when it is shared, and Andrée Putman is very good at sharing. She planted wild strawberries near the bamboo thicket and the magnolias for her grandchildren. "It's such a pleasure to watch them rush over like a flock of sparrows looking for the sweet, fragrant fruit."

A terrace with a bath

It gets very hot on this south-facing terrace in the summer, so it was partly covered by a trellis structure covered with wisteria and climbing roses. Nothing can be better than enjoying the cool, fragrant shade, especially as the wooden slats of the trellis are painted white, which makes this area look almost like a seaside resort. Furthermore, the deep blue of the large lava stone table creates the illusion of a pool in the center of the terrace.

The small upper terrace leads to a room complete with a bath and jacuzzi. This in turn opens onto a garden, planted with boxwood pruned into spheres, small maples in containers, and *Miscanthus,* a lovely ornamental grass which forms tight tufts that flower in autumn. Stones have been placed on pearlgrass, a very soft little moss that is covered with white flowers in spring. A Japanese honeysuckle covers the railing, setting off the view over the dome of the Invalides.

Below: This lovely bathroom, complete with jacuzzi, leads to the upper terrace.

Opposite: The white pergola is covered with wisteria and roses, forming a contrast with the soft gray of the wooden floorboards. To the left, the magnificent foliage of an Aralia.

Following double page: The architectural rigor of the white trellis is set off by the climbing roses and windows. It surrounds the large blue lava table. A white metal staircase leads to the upper terrace.

A rooftop pool

Above: A path of terra-cotta tiles leads through the lawn.

Opposite: Potted magnolias and camellias surround the swimming pool.

Following double page: Flowerbeds containing mahonias, azaleas, rhododendrons, and choisyas create separate areas of greenery, dominated by large trees, such as the Norwegian pine.

This terrace, on the top floor of a large building in Neuilly, is a true garden that stretches right round the apartment. The heart of the garden is a sumptuous emerald green pool. Large terra-cotta pots planted with *Magnolia grandiflora* surround the pool, creating a geometric sense of space. The foliage of *Camellia japonica* harmonizes perfectly with that of the magnolias; it grows along a white trellis with oval openings, like medallions, which create a series of enchanting views.

Pink terra-cotta slabs, placed in the lawn, lead through the garden. There are many trees here, and the flowerbeds planted under them create a illusion of depth. Umbrella pines and palms structure the beds in which bamboos, choisyas, and pink azaleas are mixed with white rhododendrons. Large-leaved hostas underneath a maple with delicately scalloped foliage spread out over the lawn; the deep green of their leaves resembles waterlilies floating on still water.

The beds create green arbors linked by little paths. The cool shade they provide beckons the visitor to rest a while and perhaps share an intimate conversation under the huge sky. Flowers grow alongside fruit trees, while white peonies and fragrant old roses, foxgloves, and elegant astilbes in various shades of pink and red, thrive under cherry, pear, and peach trees. The harvest is always awaited with a great deal of impatience—although, unfortunately, the birds sometimes get to the crops first.

The garden is hardly ever drab in the winter months because a large number of the plants are evergreen. The best moment, however, is when the bulbs start to flower: crocuses, daffodils, and wonderfully fragrant hyacinths announce a triumphant start to the spring season.

An ocean liner

Standing on this large terrace on the top floor of a building constructed by Gunsberg, who was one of Le Corbusier's students, is a little bit like being aboard an ocean liner: broad white beams structure the different linked spaces like a series of bulwarks. This powerful architectural geometry is accentuated by an imposing smokestack and the shimmering blue surface of the swimming pool.

The terrace has an abundance of flowers; the season begins with *Lavandula stoechas,* also called fairy wings or "butterfly" lavender, and winter jasmine with yellow flowers. Next to bloom are the clematis and roses, including the delightful deep pink Bourbon rose, known as "Mme Isaac Pereire."

The autumn is festive and colorful with wonderfully delicate Japanese asters and the willow-leaved veronica, *Hebe salicifolia.*

Below: The pool, flanked by a chimney, looks as though it's on the deck of an ocean liner.

Opposite: A lovely old rose, "New Dawn," blooms exuberantly, almost blocking the view of the Eiffel Tower beyond.

A play of mirrors

This apartment used to belong to Félix Houphouët-Boigny, president of the Ivory Coast, who loved the view across the rooftops of Paris. The new owners also fell in love with the place, ideally situated in the heart of the city, especially its huge terrace—which, though dotted with a forest of chimneys, still has a magnificent panoramic view.

Anxious to make the best of the strange parts of this terrace and to use modern materials, the owners came up with the idea of covering all the chimneys with mirrors to create endless reflections of the sky and views. In keeping with this aesthetic decision in favour of a resolutely contemporary design, they brought in oil drums and transformed them into large metal containers for plants.

One of the features of this terrace is that it is level with the apartment and has a smaller second floor reached by

Below: These young pear trees, growing in a fan-shaped espalier, were planted to create a windbreak.

Opposite: The sweeping view and infinite variety of the Paris sky in the early evening are reflecting in mirrors attached to the chimneys.

an aluminum staircase. A shower was installed outside, alongside a passageway that is perfect for sunbathing, as it is protected from prying eyes by a hedge of tamarisks.

The large terrace is not completely flat in the middle, but instead of trying to level everything, landscape designer Pascal Cribier decided to use the varying levels by creating a low flowerbed. "I wanted to create a orchard in the bed," says the owner, "with real fruit trees and wild plants beneath them." There is also a Judas tree and an olive tree, which grow amid a thicket of horsetails. A row of bamboos softens the sharp line at the edge of the roof. A few openings have been cut into this bamboo wall, creating a series of viewpoints like paintings inserted into a tapestry of plants. A double fan-shaped espaliered pear tree grows along one of the walls. The plants grow in excellent earth, brought here from the country; none of them have highly developed root systems, which means they do not exhaust the soil. Euphorbias and other plants from southern France, including pittosporums and silver-leafed ornamental grasses, grow alongside evergreen jasmine.

The sun shines brightly in the apartment, which is situated on a north-south axis. Additional windows, similar to medieval loopholes, were opened in the walls to create views over the urban landscape and to bring extra sunlight in throughout the day. The L-shaped terrace lies along an east-west axis and offers a majestic view over the whole of Paris. With its wide sliding doors, the apartment is both intimate and yet fully open to the outdoors. "We love this openness to the sky and the interplay of mirrors, which break up and deconstruct the light; it changes constantly. Even though glass in itself is a cold material, when it reflects the blue of the skies and the clouds, it becomes alive and loses its rigidity, and can even transmit some of this modern and warm quality to metal, to the aluminum. We are fascinated by the contrast between the plants and these materials which no longer seem cold. All our frustrations disappear when we're on this terrace."

Above: Open-air showers in the solarium.

Below: Olives and fruit trees.

Opposite: The generous forms of Macleaya cordata *at the end of the season, opposite the staircase leading to the upper terrace.*

A sky-high vegetable garden

Above: The vegetable garden with the Pompidou Center in the background.

Opposite: Christian Duc planted his vegetable plots in the midst of a bed of sedum.

This building was constructed in 1932 in the Beaubourg neighborhood by a couple who had suffered from the severe food shortages in France during World War I. They therefore planned ahead, and set up a large terrace on the top of the building that could be transformed into a vegetable garden in times of need. It has 60 centimeters (2 feet) of earth and a well-designed drainage system.

No one knows for sure if vegetables were grown on this rooftop during the German occupation. But it's certain that Christian Duc, when he rented this apartment and terrace for several years, didn't hesitate for a minute. With the help of his friend, landscape designer Pascal Cribier, he created a vegetable garden in the magnificent 160-square-meter space, which also has a spectacular view. The playful shape of the Pompidou Center, many bell-towers, a small piece of the Bastille Opera, and the skyscrapers of La Défense are all visible from the top of the building.

Their first undertaking, which they considered essential, was to build a shed to house the tools, pots, seeds, and bell-glasses. Large plots were created for the vegetables. Pascal Cribier surrounded them with sedum, which forms a huge carpet of yellow flowers in June, like a meadow in bloom. Boxwood was planted around the edges to define the paths.

Aromatic herbs, zucchini, cabbages, and salad crops sensitive to cold were planted in the square plots; they were protected from any drop in temperature by a flock of large bell-glasses. These were carefully aligned as in a small mixed garden. There were also raspberries and strawberries, used in delicious desserts. For a while, Christian Duc even kept bees, which produced wonderful honey.

Instead of using all the ground for crops, as is often the case in vegetable gardens, Pascal Cribier left a large

In the foreground, the beautiful foliage of a tree peony. A vast view of the capital stretches out beyond the bell-glasses.

open space around the vegetable plots, creating a sense of promising emptiness, which is reflected perfectly by the immensity of the sky—here, you feel more as if you're on an island than in the heart of Paris. As well as that, the vegetable plots, given that they look somewhat "wild," add to the impression of being on an island—a desert island where a solitary Robinson Crusoe cultivates just what he needs to survive and no more.

Yet solitude is not always the rule here. In the spring and summer months, the residents organize wonderful parties and relaxed picnics, as if they were in the country.

90

Few flowers or shrubs were planted. Christian Duc wanted to keep the view wide open, so Pascal Cribier kept vertical lines to a minimum, planting only Chinese tree peonies, *Paeonia suffruticosa*, which have lush, almost tropical foliage and are covered with spectacular flowers in May. Christian Duc admires these plants immensely. They remind him of far-off Asia, his native land.

A cluster of bell-glasses protects a crop of gourds.

Hanging gardens

Sometimes, when you are walking through Paris and glance up at the sky, you may be surprised to see large patches of greenery embellishing the rooftops. Once you start to pay attention, you'll be amazed at how many there are. This vegetable mosaic is the sign of a mysterious parallel universe, one of hanging gardens inhabited by birds, flowers, and trees—jungles of bamboo, cascading honeysuckle, and babbling fountains.

Glass walls

Part of the roof of this former industrial building was raised to create a well of light, enclosed by a series of glass walls that set off a patio in the center. All the rooms in the apartments face this central patio. Giant bamboos grow up from the floor below, emerging in the center. It doesn't matter that their roots are deep in the cellar, as long as the foliage can breathe and receives sufficient light. The glass walls around the patio are used as supports for ivy and Virginia creeper; their leaves soften the sunlight and create a luxuriant atmosphere in the rooms.

The beauty of this spot lies in the use of vertical lines and sloping glass panels to structure the space. The glass creates an interplay of reflections which, with the effect of daylight on the foliage, gives an aerial lightness to the entire apartment. The metal structures are painted black; green and black harmonize well together to create a restful setting.

Fairly young olive trees were planted in containers; it took some time for them to settle in, but now they seem to have become acclimatized to their growing conditions. The lovely gray-green leaves with silver highlights add an additional nuance to the wide range of greens that dominate the patio.

The patio has sun throughout much of the day. In the morning, it shines into the bedrooms; in the afternoon, the light is softened a little by shadows. The patio is not lit at night, but it is softly illuminated by the light from the rooms around it, creating an intimate atmosphere.

Plants are a constant presence here and are part of every aspect of life in this home. An imposing green pool table in the large living room links the interior space with the outdoors. The same impression of calm and peace reigns throughout.

Page 92: A forest of bamboo, suspended on the rooftop of a Paris building.

Above: A thicket of giant bamboo, in the heart of a patio encircled by Virginia creeper.

Opposite: The large glass-walled living room is bathed in the luxurious light that filters through the plants.

Following double page: The glass walls act as supports for ivy and Virginia creeper, the large leaves of which contrast with the ethereal foliage of the giant bamboo. Two olive trees planted in pots add a gentle silver-gray tone to the garden.

Ferns and bamboos

This terrace, designed by the landscape gardener Robert Bazelaire, is constructed over a parking lot and is surrounded by high walls. It looks like a secret forest, bathed in a soft light that filters through gaps between the leaves. The house is built along one of the walls. Large sliding glass windows lead to the terrace. The major advantage here is that nothing directly over-looks this garden. The high walls protect it from prying eyes, and the owners enjoy total privacy. On the other hand, even though the terrace faces directly south, it unfortunately only gets sun for a few short hours dur-ing the daytime.

Robert Bazelaire wanted to make maximum use of what could have been a handicap—the lack of sun—so he came up with the idea of creating a bamboo forest on this terrace. Indeed, bamboo grows well in the shade provided that it gets enough sunlight for its leaves. He also planted large ferns under the bamboos and a ground cover of helxine. A Japanese-style building placed at the back of the garden looks like a tea pavilion. A few bamboo stalks were painted in strong colors (bamboo is the only plant that can be painted without being dam-aged): black for dusk; yellow for the light that filters in; and deep red for the leaves of maple trees, camellia flowers, and male dogwoods. Different varieties of climbing roses and clematis, which do particularly well in partially shaded areas, grow along the walls. They were all selected for the various shades of their white flowers, which are luminous in the gentle light of the terrace and stand out in the soft filtered sunlight. The pale green helxine ground cover looks like a carpet of moss and is extremely smooth underfoot. A few birch trees, with white trunks and pale foliage, harmonize well with the svelte bamboo stalks and create a similar sense of translucence.

Above: Bamboo is the only plant that can be painted, because it breathes through its leaves and not its stem. The bright yellow adds a vivid touch to the dusky light that reigns here.

Opposite: The tea pavilion, nestling in a thicket of bamboo, separates the terrace into two separate gardens. The ferns in the foreground form a gentle contrast with the sharp outlines of the painted bamboo. An evergreen Camellia sasanqua *in the background flowers in the autumn.*

To reinforce the impression of being in forest undergrowth, Robert Bazelaire created the illusion of a river by constructing a wooden bridge over a bed of different sized bolders. A cover under this bridge slides open to reveal a jacuzzi. "We bathe here all year round," says the owner, "even when it snows."

A multitude of factors contribute to the charming atmosphere of calm and meditation: the dusky filtered light; the soft ground cover formed by a carpet of helxine and the elegant, delicate foliage of ferns; as well as the refined choice of colors. The interplay of light and shadow created by the plants is accompanied by the gentle rustling of leaves, which move with the slightest breeze. This garden makes you feel as if you've stepped into a Corot painting, complete with a dreamlike forest bathed in pale, silvery light.

Below left: Helxine grows between and over the stones that form a small staircase, while a rhododendron borders it to the right.

Below right: Birch trees and bamboo form an intimate, poetic setting.

Opposite: The jacuzzi garden with its sliding bridge. The clump of birch trees and bamboo and the foliage of Cornus controversa are reflected in the glass windows. Royal ferns (Osmunda regalis) cover the ground.

A peaceful jungle

Almost every house in this private road in the 7th *arrondissement* has its own garden. This one, which is practically at the end of the street, has a terrace on the roof of a garage, designed twenty years ago by Robert Bazelaire. It was nothing more than a narrow patch of shade, very close to ground level, with walls on both sides of it. "A hole," remembers Robert Bazelaire. "What is amazing is that, even in a hole, you can put in a large number of plants. I started by planting giant bamboos here; they create an illusion of impenetrable depth. I compensated for the lack of space on the ground by using the vertical height."

A few steps lead to a small stone-paved terrace outside the living room and dining room of the house. A long, beautiful, Indian stone is placed on the edge of the terrace. It was probably designed to channel and collect rainwater, and has become a symbol of this garden by transforming it into a timeless Asian jungle. The pure lines of the stone, combined with the strange light in the garden, form a meditative setting that seems to be impervious to any outside influences.

This garden has not changed since it was first designed. With the stone and bamboo, it looks as though it has been here for ever. The ethereal foliage catches sunlight in such as way as to look like a fine dusting of gold. The idea of alternating spaces of light and dark is very appealing; it is like the moment when a rainy sky starts to clear and the sun comes out. This garden emanates a feeling of tranquility, punctuated by the rustling of leaves and the calls of a few blackbirds who have settled in the bamboos. It is a delicate sound, with many subtleties if you take the time to listen.

Fallen leaves cover the ground. A handful of cut bamboo branches stand in a corner, near one of the walls enclosing the terrace. The overall effect looks like a piece of Land Art.

Above: A bed of fallen leaves is scattered under the bamboo, alongside a stone purchased in India and placed on a support sculpted by Robert Bauzelaire.

Opposite: A small sitting area on the terrace is bathed in soft light, filtered through the bamboo leaves.

Following double page: Small chestnut trees grow like bonsai in a large oval pot in front of the living room and under the bamboo stalks. In the foreground, the large stone evokes the stones in Indian temples that are used to collect rainwater.

An exotic retreat

Above: The strange flowers of Acanthus mollis *grow among the lovely green and yellow-spotted foliage of an* Aralia.

Opposite: A small wooden bridge spans a bed of stones in the foreground; to the right is a thicket of bamboo; to the left, a clump of Miscanthus sinensis, *an ornamental grass that has remarkable foliage of yellow and green.* Hydrangea quercifolia *produces lovely white flowers.*

A wide variety of foliage creates the impression of being in some far-off land, rather than on this luxurious terrace perched on top of a modern building in the 15th *arrondissement.* The veranda outside the apartment was transformed into a winter garden; the terrace, according to the owner's wishes, is covered with flourishing plants. The space was designed by landscape gardener Alain-Charles as a series of alcoves defined by beds; in the center is a wooden bridge over a river of stones.

The plants in the beds were selected for the beauty of their form, their unique foliage, or the fragrance of their flowers. Small-leafed bamboos grow alongside large clumps of acanthus; an *Aralia* with large, deeply scalloped leaves spotted yellow and green; and a *Nandina,* or sacred bamboo, with purple leaves and red berries in October and November. A *Yucca flaccida,* with long green and yellow leaves, creates a lovely contrast alongside *Viburnum tinus,* which has fragrant flowers during the winter. Near the small bridge, a tuft of bamboo grouped with *Miscanthus sinesis,* a gracious ornamental grass whose green leaves are edged in yellow, forms a poetic composition evoking a Far-Eastern landscape. Birch trees add a lighter note to the dark areas of the terrace, as does *Ligustrum,* or Chinese privet, which is covered with large panicles of small, fragrant, white flowers in spring. Lavender and clumps of lilies are dotted around the terrace, along with a few annuals such as balsams and anemones.

A pretty bench offers a place to rest in the shade. *Cornus kousa* and rhododendrons with white flowers grow along the length of the house. The back of the terrace is bordered with trees and shrubs: olive trees, cypress, pittosporum with white leaves speckled with gray and green, and pink and white azaleas.

Narrow paths

Emmy de Martaelere and her husband had a great idea after seeing scaffolding be put up during resurfacing work along the side of their building: once the work was finished, they decided to keep the horizontal surface and transform it into a long narrow terrace for a hanging garden. Covered with wood flooring, this improvised terrace was meant to be just a temporary structure. Several years later it is still in place, and the roses and bignonias that were planted in pots have now covered large stretches of the wall. As for the railing, it is completely covered with ivy and honeysuckle.

"I have exceptional azaleas in the largest containers," says Emmy de Martaelere. "They are more than one meter (three feet) in diameter when they bloom. They flower for about three weeks and, because they don't all bloom at the same time, we enjoy them for a long period. Initially, the flowers were pink, although paler than I would have liked. By adding iron to the water, I managed to get them to take on a very warm shade of brick red."

She also has several lovely boxwoods that she prunes into round shapes. In the art of topiary, as in drawing, the eye is as important as the hand. With a bit of practice, you can achieve almost perfect forms. The bignonias must also be pruned regularly or they will quickly overrun their space. They are perfect for hiding unsightly walls: the long branches, which end with bouquets of trumpet-shaped orange-red flowers, have leafy tendrils that wind around supports.

A row of pots lined up along the wall that gets the most sun has a large variety of seasonal flowers. The roses produce enough flowers for bouquets throughout the house. Despite its narrow width, this terrace is big enough for several chaises longues for lazy afternoons in the sun.

Above: A potful of marguerites at the base of a small wooden staircase adds a light touch to a rather dark corner.

Opposite: Two magnificent azaleas occupy pride of place on the wooden floor that stretches between the walls—which are covered with bignonias and climbing roses.

Balcony with ginkgo

After Christian Duc had transformed his rooftop terrace into a vegetable garden, he decided to change apartments—and scale. His space is now smaller, but he still created a miniature hanging garden on his balcony. He first planted trees to create a sense of depth; these include a Japanese apple, a liquidambar, a ginkgo, and a double-flowered lilac, surrounded by a variety of different ferns. He chose old plants, which have survived any number of catastrophes, such as the ginkgo, the first tree to reappear in Hiroshima, and horsetails, which date from prehistoric times. His minuscule garden is a tiny timeline, similar to the landscape of northern Asia, a region he knows well.

In the spring, the apple tree is covered in a cloud of white flowers; in the autumn, the leaves are red and gold. A few perennials—hydrangeas and hostas—grow in large pots.

Below: A gilded Buddha just inside the windows seems to protect the serene atmosphere of the apartment.

Opposite: A few flowers—primroses, hostas, and a hydrangea—grow on the balcony in the shade of Ginkgo biloba, *the tree with a hundred shield-shaped leaves.*

Oases in
the sky

Some people put so much care into their
hanging gardens that they are transformed
into real outdoor living areas. These are
timeless spaces, decorated with statues,
unusual pieces of furniture and multicolored
carpets of vegetation. These places exist
in a state of suspended animation, where
the heady scent of old roses fills the air
as the sun sets behind the domes and
towers of Paris's monuments—which
stand out like Chinese silhouettes against
the darkening sky.

Arches and greenhouses

Camille Muller is responsible for the design of this outdoor living space on a large terrace that takes up the entire roof of a modern building in Neuilly. What appears to be chaos is actually a technically complex creation. Nothing was left to chance, and the natural charm of this space is the result of a skillful combination of imagination and expertise. The apartment belongs to an industrialist who loves nature. He bought it when it was still in its planning stages, and Camille Muller defined the organization of the space on paper, working with a rare degree of freedom: more often landscape designers have to work within the existing constraints of a building, trying to make the most of what he or she has at hand.

Arches of trellis divide the space into various sections. The design takes into account a number of setbacks along the central walk, which is covered with wooden planks. A veranda, against which a large bench has been placed, has an interesting feature: strands of ivy underscore its structural lines. What seems at first glance to be a simple way of dressing up the glass window, a sort of afterthought in the overall décor, is in fact the basis for the entire design. It is this idea that determined the arrangement of the glass panels, defined by a series of lines of plants. To ensure that the branches of ivy would remain exactly in the most elegant place, according to a rigorous plan, they had to be attached to a hand-made metal sheath. A blacksmith was also hired to make the guard rail, which was modeled after a type of railing used in old greenhouses. It runs along the top of the veranda and the adjoining buildings, adding a romantic note to this small corner of nature. This impression is reinforced by a wooden fence framed by pruned boxwood, which looks as though it leads to an open field. Everything looks natural here, and the harmonious relationship

Trellis covered with ivy encloses the wooden terrace, where benches, a table, and armchairs create a pleasant outdoor sitting room in the midst of viburnum, roses, and escallonias.

between the plants and the objects placed on the terrace seems to have been formed over years. The plants look as though they have grown here almost spontaneously. This natural appearance is, however, a total illusion, created by a subtle interplay between the different levels, which are used to conceal the earth and the watering systems while creating the best growing conditions for the plants.

The terrace faces east and southwest and has sun throughout the day. On one side are a series of willows, *Salix exigua*, a loquat tree, and roses, including "Mermaid," a climbing variety with large pale yellow flowers and protruding sulfur-yellow stamens. On the west side is

ironwood (*Parrotia persica*), a small tree originally from the Caucasus, which has white flowers and long red anthers. It grows alongside a Noisette rose, "Aimée Vibert," which is covered with superb clusters of small, pure-white flowers; several escallonias with pink flowers; viburnums and arbutus; and evergreen shrubs, with a naturally luxuriant appearance. Dense vegetation—ivy and "Fée des neiges" roses—covers the arbor facing the veranda on the opposite side of the garden.

Although this terrace is the result of complex planning, it looks so natural that even the architecture appears to be made of plants.

A Prunus and a Cornus florida rise skyward on the balcony, which looks like an observatory or the deck of a ship.

A baroque living room

This apartment, near the Bois de Boulogne, faces a terrace designed as a lovely outdoor sitting room. Sheltered by a wall of trees—birch, maple (*Acer palmatum*), and pieris—the garden protects the visitor against any intrusion from the outside world. Even the sky is partially concealed by the foliage. The 1930s garden furniture is made of cement, cast to look like wood; it adds a sophisticated cachet to the garden that the owner, who collects art objects, is particularly fond of.

The garden is carefully maintained, but, unlike an English lawn, the grass is dotted with a cheerful sprinkling of daisies and buttercups.

Designed with a backdrop of evergreen trees and shrubs, this garden changes colors several times a year: the pieris turn red and orange in the spring; the maples are a sumptuous garnet color in autumn; and the dwarf petunias and other seasonal flowers contribute bright summer colors.

Below: A table and chairs in front of the dining room window form a second small sitting room, under the shade of the Japanese maple trees (Acer japonicum).

Opposite: The 1930s garden furniture, cast in concrete to imitate wood, is placed near a small grove of birch trees.

Following double page: Playful mushroom-shaped sculptures emerge from the flowerbeds planted with Mexican orange trees (choisyas) and daphnes.

Second-hand style

Élisabeth Brac de La Perrière has two passions: sec-
ond-hand objects and gardens, two activities that
are, in fact, fairly similar. The pleasure in unearthing an
old copper basin or discovering an almost forgotten
variety of old rose is identical.

This terrace occupies the entire roof of a modern
building in Neuilly. There was no earth here, so everything is planted in pots and containers, with a drip
watering system. The plants were selected according to
the northeast exposure and the ever-present wind.
Cooler tones—greens, blues, and gray—dominate the
color scheme with lavender, rosemary, thyme, and
pruned boxwood, while rhododendrons, azaleas, and
hydrangeas contribute softer shades. The various greens
of the foliage create a backdrop for rustic objects placed
around the outdoor sitting room: watering cans, bell-
glasses, and roof finials.

*Below: A collection of zinc watering cans,
roof finials, and bell-glasses contribute to the
individual style of this flower-filled terrace.*

*Opposite: An amusing collection of old watering
cans near the potted lavender and azaleas.*

A scholar's refuge

Above: A view of the hanging garden from the balcony; it looks like a island covered with plants, complete with an arbor entirely concealed under a mauve wisteria.

Opposite: A romantic stone path leads to a secret garden. The stone slabs are edged with a bed of helxine, hostas, and elephant ear ferns, along with a bronze sculpture by Poles, placed opposite an imposing Taxus × media *"Strait Hedge."*

He wears green suits the color of oak leaves, hinting at a link with the gardens he has always loved. The one he designed around his home in Saint-Florent, Corsica, is enchanting. His Paris terrace was created in partnership with the famous English landscape designer Russell Page. He spends a lot of time in this garden, an extension of his Paris apartment.

This terrace resembles an island suspended from the top of the building. It looks out over several beautiful gardens in the capital, including that of the British Embassy, which is filled with magnificent trees. The terrace runs alongside several bedrooms and the office and is enclosed by a railing covered with a beautiful mauve-colored wisteria. Openings between the trees and shrubs that offer pretty views of the gardens below.

A series of terra-cotta pots filled with boxwood is arranged along the railing, while a Virginia creeper climbs up a black trellis attached to the pale yellow rough-cast walls.

Three steps framed by large round boxwood shrubs lead to the second section of the terrace, which is somewhat behind the apartment. Large stone slabs form a path, lined with helxine, hostas, and elephant ear ferns (*Elaphoglossum crinitum*), which have bright red highlights in the autumn. At ground level, the eyes are drawn to the generous form of a bronze sculpture of a woman.

A thick bed of fragrant choisyas (Mexican orange) surrounds a thicket of Irish yew, *Taxus baccata* "Fastigiata." A great sense of calm reigns in this secret poetic hideaway. The grass follows the curve of the path that leads to a Baroque bench by Müller. It stands in front of a hedge of pruned privet, under the shade of a maple tree.

This hanging garden is, of course, at its best in the springtime. A number of the rooms have large glass

doors leading to the garden, so the terrace and the plants are closely linked to the rhythm of daily life inside the apartment. In the winter, the bare branches form interesting visual effects, and so does the gradual appearance of buds and tiny leaves in the spring—the leaves offer quantities of shades of green, for example, the pale green of the wisteria and the darker green of the boxwood.

There are other connecting factors between the interior and outdoors: a few contemporary works of art inhabit the terrace, including a piece by Tinguely. These are part of a larger art collection brought together by Maurice Rheims, a modern art aficionado; most of the works are on display in the apartment, providing the same lively sense of companionship inside as the plants do outside.

Below left: A contemporary polychrome bronze on the trellis.

Below right: A bronze by Poles, surrounded by elephant ear ferns.

Opposite: Breaks in the magnificent wisteria offer different views over the city.

A winter garden

This terrace looks like a little piece of the Parc Montsouris. The park is just across the street and, as the apartment is higher up, the terrace is at the same level as the lush foliage of the treetops. The view over the park is quite simply spectacular. There are no buildings in sight, and the view extends unobstructed over the grass as if it were the surface of a pond. The most extraordinary time of the day is when the park is closed to the public, early in the morning or at night, when the only sound is that of birdsong.

The terrace and its raised edges are covered with wood planking. Everything is planted in pots and containers, like the superb clumps of daisies that grow alongside the roses. The ledges are covered with ivy, mixed with pots of geranium and small shrubs trained as standards. The park seems to start right on this terrace.

The owner is fond of an oriental lifestyle and set up the simplest and most creative garden area possible: it consists of just a large carpet and cushions with a few candle lamps. She entertains her friends or spends long hours reading here.

The Parisian climate does not always lends itself to open-air living, however, so she transformed the veranda extending from the apartment into a conservatory. It stands out against the wall of the adjoining ivy-clad building, where a number of birds have nested. A bench and a few chaises longues made of wooden slats, placed in front of the veranda, catch any bit of sunlight.

The owner loves the style of her terrace and is thinking of cloaking the veranda, which is not very appealing as it is, in a sort of Turkish tent. The problem is finding something simple, easy to install, amusing and especially tasteful, in keeping with the exotic atmosphere she has created.

Among the trees

The architect Bruno de Panafieu lives in a complex of artists' studios constructed on the site of a former warehouse. His studio has two linked terraces overlooking a large garden. The blue tiles on the walls remind him of Portugal and his childhood. Bruno de Panafieu travels regularly throughout Africa, and he brings back seeds and plants that he acclimatizes on his terrace, such as cactuses, hibiscus plants from Mali, and a banana tree. He developed a technique of folding banana leaves, which he uses to create sculptures and jewelry, and even sturdy boxes.

These tropical plants fit in perfectly with the other vegetation, an Austrian pine or a prunus, for example, whose deep red rivals that of the maples. During warm weather, garden furniture is placed on the terrace, which is in full bloom with lilacs, photinias, forsythias, yellow roses, Scotch broom, honeysuckle, and oleanders.

Below: Climbing roses, jasmine, photinias, and forsythias grow in containers around the 1930s-style butterfly chairs. The ocher-colored walls add a warm note.

Opposite: A bird's-eye view through the foliage of a Davidia of the terrace below, with its mugo pine (Pinus mugo).

Labyrinths

This immense terrace on the top of a building with a view of the Eiffel Tower was designed by Robert Bazelaire. The aim was to create a real garden, inspired by the landscape of Tuscany. The L-shaped terrace is quite long and has several levels. Robert Bazelaire is both a landscape designer and an accomplished botanist; here, he designed stone slab paths lined with lavender and a remarkable collection of dogwoods: a *Cornus controversa,* or giant dogwood, with variegated foliage; a *Cornus kousa,* a small tree that is covered in pure white flowers in June; and a *Cornus florida,* which has a myriad of small pink and cream-white flowers in May. The pittosporums, which have a fragrance similar to that of jasmine, form a hedge that draws the eye toward the slender cypress trees and the thujas. Everything is pruned and structured, in keeping with the Italian influence, but there is also a profusion of flowers, such as roses, honeysuckle, and passion flowers.

Below: The sitting area of the terrace, with a white parasol and tiled path, is lined with maples, lavender, an Azalea japonica, a Magnolia stellata, and a Cotoneaster franchetii.

Opposite: A succession of stone slabs in the grass is lined with beds of lavender and Juniperus horizontalis. It leads to the sitting area, over which rise the slender forms of Florentine cypress trees.

Open-air dining

Eating outdoors is a wonderful experience.
Added to the fun of being outside is the
magic of the terrace or hanging garden itself,
and the pleasure of such an experience right in
the heart of the city. Dining at a simple table set
up under an arbor or enjoying a sophisticated
meal served in a party setting is always a special
occasion, something like being on a desert island,
far from the hubbub of the city below.

Dinner is served

Page 136: Boxwood pruned into spheres or topiary shapes frame this outdoor dining room, which is used as much as possible during warm weather.

Above: The long black metal table against the terrace balustrade is ready for a candlelit dinner. The pine tree in the background echoes the stately line of trees lining the avenue below. Tufts of lavender grow around its trunk.

Opposite: The floral decoration on the table this evening is of Mediterranean inspiration. The orange and yellow flowers —an evergreen jasmine to the left, a bougainvillea to the right—match the dishes and hors d'œuvres set out for the start of a meal.

The architect and decorator Serge Robin lives near the Eiffel Tower on Avenue Rapp, in an apartment with a large terrace arranged as a small patch of the hinterland Provence, covered with jasmine, lavender, and umbrella pine trees.

Serge Robin works on projects all over the world and travels to the Middle East, Asia, Africa, and Latin America. Many friends from abroad come to visit, and he likes to explore various styles of entertaining and arranging his table during the receptions he organizes on the terrace. He is well suited to the task: he is the designer for Art de la Table in Paris and organizes exhibitions on this theme in Tokyo and New York. The décor for these events is always different, yet they are all based on a single rule, which is to link the space outdoors with the interior, the terrace with the apartment. This apartment is decorated in tones of bluish-gray, copper, and deep red. The terrace counters this scheme with gray-greens, silver and the blue-gray lavender—offset in the summer by the bright pink and orange bougainvillea. "It's a real pleasure for me," confides Serge Robin. "I always try to create a new variation on the theme of the relationship between colors. It's like theater or set design. My friends love the festive ambience that fills the apartment as it opens up to the outdoors, with the view over Paris and the magic of the Eiffel Tower illuminated at night. You may not like some of the architectural designs of our time, but you have to admit that the illumination of the Parisian monuments is splendid."

This terrace has been the setting for many a party, but it is also a place of rest, which Serge Robin appreciates even more after returning home from a business trip. On one side is the view of the Eiffel Tower, and on the other, the Champs-de-Mars. He never takes this for granted and still enjoys it as much as ever.

Under a sunshade

It's a great pleasure to lunch beneath a sunshade on the roof of a building in the Marais. At one time, there was a small factory here that manufactured uniforms for policemen. Today, the house has been restored and once again has the charm that is so characteristic of the neighborhood. The penthouse apartment has a veranda, which faces a large terrace designed by Robert Bazelaire. The landscape designer decided to enclose the terrace with a wall of plants to make it more private. He played with contrasts and used different types of foliage to create a sense of depth: in the foreground are the shiny leaves of rhododendrons and camellias; in the background, the slender, ethereal leaves of bamboo. Maple trees, with lovely divided leaves, grow in large containers in between the two. The white and red camellias add a note of color.

Below: An overall view of the terrace with a sunshade—which protects people from the sun and from prying eyes—and the small outdoor dining room. The elegance of the terrace comes from the sober décor and the harmonious use of wood and metal.

Opposite: The table is set for a summer dinner, near a thicket of bamboo and a maple (in the foreground to the right).

Flowers and foliage

Above: A pretty collection of spring flowers grow in pots on this small table: hyacinths, daffodils, grape hyacinths.

Opposite: An outdoor dining room; a cotoneaster grows at the base of an ivy-clad wall. A lovely willow provides shade in the background.

Designed by landscape architect Alain Richert, Christiane and Éric Germain's terrace is a garden of green, highlighted with numerous spots of bright color. The terrace is just outside the living room of these art collectors. As soon the weather is warm enough, they lunch and dine outdoors.

There used to be a convent and a vineyard in this neighborhood in the 15th *arrondissement*. It felt very much like a village. It has changed a great deal, but nature is still present everywhere: many buildings have private gardens. Christiane and Éric Germain's terrace overlooks a large garden, which is especially nice in that no wall or enclosure separates the two spaces. The property line is marked simply by a row of plants. The depth of vision is therefore wide and from the terrace they can fully enjoy the greenery of the nearby trees and foliage.

Space is fairly limited on the terrace itself, so the landscape designer put in a large number of plants, creating an overall impression of charming Bohemian clutter. A climbing hydrangea, *Hydrangea petiolaris,* grows up the trellis on the walls. In England, climbing hydrangeas are popular for many qualities: they have fragrant, small white flowers that stand out beautifully from their light green leaves, which turn to golden shades in the autumn.

Christiane and Éric Germain love scented plants, so there are several types of jasmine, including *Jasminun nudiflorum,* which blooms in winter at the same time as *Clematis sirrhosa* "Freckles" and *Camellia sasanqua.* Nothing is lovelier that the sight of these flowers in bloom during a cold, gray Paris winter. The roses bloom next, with the sumptuous "Madame Isaac Pereire," which has dark pink flowers edged in magenta, and the famous climbing Noisette "Gloire de Dijon," with delicately scented ocher-yellow flowers.

Two plants with evergreen foliage, rhododendrons and viburnums, are planted in beds which form a border around the terrace. The elegant viburnum has honey-scented pink or white flowers throughout most of the winter season. Other fragrant flowers grow in pots placed near the flowerbeds, including a collection of hostas with green or variegated foliage and small blue or large white flowers; violets; and quantities of flowering bulbs such as hyacinths, daffodils, and small grape hyacinths.

The terrace also has a number of perennials, offering a nest of greenery for the many birds that take refuge here in the winter months. "We love listening to the birds fight over their territory in the evening, just as the sun starts to set," confides Christiane Germain. "They announce the coming of the night."

Below left: The beautiful flower of Helleborus orientalis *and its cluster of stamens.*

Below right: A daffodil just about to bloom.

Opposite: A collection of potted hostas: Hosta fortunei *with variegated foliage, and* Hosta sieboldiana, *with ribbed green or blue-green leaves.*

A play of shadows

Above: The summer dining room, with a wood floor, is shaded by a horizontal awning. Oleanders, standard roses, and a lemon tree grow in large pots.

Opposite: A series of terraces overlook the garden, which is shaded by a pagoda tree (Sophorica japonica).

Following double page: The outdoor dining room seems to be suspended in the treetops.

This architect's home has terraces that extend over three levels and overlook a private garden. Situated in the middle of a block in the 5th *arrondissement,* the house faces directly south. The three terraces can be reached from the living areas and are connected by ladders on the outside. The problem here is not the lack of enough light; on the contrary, the owners have created more shade as protection from the intense sunlight.

The large pagoda tree (*Sophora japonica*) in the garden provides light shade for the second terrace, which also has contemporary horizontal sunshades for even more shelter. This terrace is an extension of the living room. The owners often eat here in the spring and summer, when they feel as though they are perching in the treetops. The sun shines gently on the wooden planks of the flooring. The oleanders, climbing roses, and jasmine, planted in large pots set along the edge of the terrace, also provide cool shade. The wall that extends from one terrace to the next is covered with a lovely green Virginia creeper that turns red and gold in the autumn.

The bedrooms on the top floor face the third terrace. This is a spare playroom for the children, who spend a great deal of time here. The ground-floor terrace, outside the offices of the architectural firm, has not been landscaped and seems to be almost bare of vegetation in comparison to the others. Nevertheless, the people working in the office still appreciate the open natural space.

Breakfasts in the cool morning air are special occasions in the springtime. During the summer, when the large garden is illuminated and the light from a few candles plays with the shadows on the terrace, the hosts and their guests spend many long hours lingering over dinner and conversation.

A terrace with perspective

Above: A collection of herbs is lined up on a shelf near the trellis enclosing the terrace. Dwarf tomato plants grow in a frame in the foreground.

Opposite: Mediterranean plants grow well on the sunny terrace; these include a fig tree, a medlar, oleanders, and hydrangeas with blue flowers. The outdoor dining room is in the background, under the sunshade. In the foreground, an ivy plant trained into a bird shape on a topiary frame.

When the owners of this old building in the 3rd *arrondissement* selected their apartment, they were attracted to several of its qualities: the beauty of the seventeenth-century painted ceilings, of course, but also the fact that the former courtyard had been covered over to create a real terrace.

The simplest but least interesting idea would have been to create a miniature French-style garden, in keeping with the classical design of the building. But this type of garden depends on the use of perspective and large expanses of space. The owners therefore decided to encircle their terrace with a line of containers, and include just a single reference to the great age of French gardens by creating a vista that leads to a beautiful seventeenth-century fountain. This was an elegant way to pay tribute to the spirit of the building while creating an intimate and natural design. The overall effect is underscored by the small sunshade and metal garden furniture, which are ideal for simple dinners outdoors.

The terrace is well sheltered, so the owners, who also have a home in the south of France, were able to bring back plants that they grow in large containers: a fig tree, a medlar tree, oleanders, and on the trellis, a combination of ivy and Virginia creeper. Red, pink, and white penstemons grow in pots throughout the year, alongside abutilons—which come from the same family as lavateras—and lantanas, which have brightly colored flowers.

Still more flowers bloom on this terrace: a mauve lilac, "Iceberg" roses, and winter-flowering camellias (*Camellia japonica* "Sea Foam" and *Camellia sasanqua*). An ivy plant, trained onto a bird-shaped frame, adds an amusing touch to these flowers that grow so informally.

A summer dining room

This tiny terrace is in a large house situated in the 7th *arrondissement* and was designed by Olivia Putman (Andrée Putman's daughter) for Florence Grinda. Blue is the dominant color, a romantic reminder that faience of this color was once made here. The building was then transformed into a residence with an lovely oriental-style garden on the ground floor. The wooden trellis on the small terrace was painted in a shade of blue so as to harmonize with the blue tiles on the outside walls. A table in mauve and pale blue ceramic designed by the Austrian artist Frederik Takenberg is the center piece of the terrace. The back wall, framed by faience panels, is decorated with a *trompe-l'œil* design that represents an oriental façade, echoing the surprising exotic garden below. The trellis is planted with jasmine, old roses, and blue, white, and mauve clematis on the trellis.

Below: An intimate setting, complete with a potted blue hydrangea and candles.

Opposite: Blue is the dominant tone of the summer dining room, echoing the blue faience tiles on the outdoor walls of the building. On the back wall is a trompe-l'œil *façade.*

Designer terraces

The terraces designed by architects and artists such as Mallet-Stevens, Jean-Pierre Raynaud, and Yves de La Tour d'Auvergne are worlds unto themselves, as unique as their owners. Each one took possession of his or her own space, which was deconstructed, sculpted, and modeled to create a jealously guarded and exceptional mode of expression between the earth and the sky.

Nature reconstructed

Jean-Pierre Raynaud has always been interested in nature, which is one of his major inspirations; indeed, he started out as a gardener. The terrace that occupies part of the roof of his house, most of which is buried underground, demonstrates this link between nature and art.

It is dominated by a type of mastaba (a flat-roofed building with sloping walls) covered with white ceramic tiles, in front of which stands an oversized red pot. There are strong contrasts wherever you look: between white and red, between the tiles and the wood—in other words, between warm and cold materials—between mineral and vegetable, and between the outsized pot and the miniature bonsai trees. Everything is squared off here, cut out and marked; everything is organized according to an interplay of contrasts that governs the design of the terrace, determines its style, and underscores the aesthetic mastery of the space. What interests the artist in the art of bonsai is the fact of controlling growth by means of pruning, in other words, a way of mastering time and space by repeated pruning. Bonsai are symbols of death (cutting back, incessant pruning) and life (knots, which are the stigmata of repeated trimming, are sources of energy). There is no life without death, interruptions, and cuts; no duration or beauty without fragility; no art without extreme contrasts. Furthermore, "I love them as much even when they die," says Jean-Pierre Raynaud, "because in their forms, they carry within them the persistent image of time. Bonsai is the dream of the Great Tree." There is something conceptual in the forms of bonsai trees, an art form in which Jean-Pierre Raynaud excels. It is the form that determines the object, by which it becomes art. You get the sense that this somewhat morbid sculptural style freezes time, while on the other hand, the plant world brings an aesthetic sense and life to it.

Page 154: The minimalist style of a contemporary terrace, lined with a cloth guardrail and 1940s butterfly chairs.

Above: The round forms of pruned boxwood frame the glass floor that is actually the roof of the house. In the background are several bonsai trees, arranged on shelves and sheltered from direct sunlight by window shades.

Opposite: This dead though majestic bonsai is the perfect image of the Great Tree.

Following double page: Jean-Pierre Raynaud's terrace reflects his art, with ubiquitous terra-cotta flowerpots and white ceramic tiles.

Boxwood topiary

This apartment has three terraces. In the owner's words, "it is like a ship with three decks." The space is dynamic; every room faces the terraces and everything is linked—the living room, dining room, and bedrooms—by a series of sliding wood or translucent glass tile partitions. There is no break between the inside and the outside. Indeed, the terraces are not closed off from the outside world beyond. They are only slightly cut off by a white wood trellis with large squares, which does not interfere with the view over the city.

This space belongs to a fashion designer whose professional life consists of presenting collections and cutting out clothes. Once he is at home, he fills his leisure moments by cutting the topiary boxwood on his terraces. He derives the same pleasure from pruning these plants as he does from making clothes. Pruning a plant into a specific shape means imposing a form and putting limits on nature, but it is also a way of respecting it, by respecting its vitality and plasticity. The boxwoods, planted in large pots or containers, are lined up along the trellis enclosure. The shiny dark green leaves form a magnificent contrast to the white of the trellis. The boxwood alternates with yew, small bamboos with slender foliage, and large clumps of white petunias.

The upper terrace is the "lighthouse," with a 360-degree, unimpeded view over Paris. It is also a solarium, where the owner and his guests can enjoy sunbathing without any intrusion. It really feels as if you are sailing in space, in the company of swallows, sparrows, blackbirds, and clouds.

"Living on a terrace is not only having extra space," says the owner, "it's also a different way of life, a more serene way of looking at time, a more distant relationship with the ups and downs of life. I am at home in this space; the inside and outside belong to me in the same way."

Above: A ceramic wheelbarrow from Sainte-Radogonde, in Provence, is used as a planter for white petunias.

Opposite: Pruned boxwood and the Taxus "Strait Hedge" to the right are planted in large containers that also come from Sainte-Radogonde.

A Mallet-Stevens terrace

Above: A view looking down at the checkerboard, marked off with pruned boxwood at each corner.

Opposite: At one end of the terrace a fountain, decorated with a large ocher and black mosaic, rises at the base of the turret. Large pots filled with azaleas, rhododendrons, birch trees, and maples stand near the guardrail.

The terrace on top of this building, constructed in 1932, looks like the deck of a ship. It was designed by Mallet-Stevens, then restored with great care by Mme. Hoffman, a decorator who has lived here for a number of years. Unfortunately, very few of the terraces designed by Mallet-Stevens still exist. Yet they bear witness to the exceptional artistic movement known as Art Deco. It also reminds us of the fascination these architects had with the era of ocean liners, symbols of luxury, and with the latest technology.

The terrace floor was paved with white ceramic tiles and, in the center, a large red and black ceramic checkerboard, set off with pruned boxwood at each corner. At the base of the turret overlooking the terrace—which houses the building's chimneys—is a fountain and a small waterfall. It is decorated with a geometric mosaic pattern in black and ocher tones and is formed by a stack of different rectangles. It looks something like the images of buildings made by Constructivist artists.

The color contrasts are repeated on the metal handrails: those on the upper levels around the chimneys are black, while the rails on the lower level are white. Terra-cotta pots filled with orange azaleas, red-leaved maples, and pink rhododendrons stand in lines around the edge of the terrace. The formal style of this terrace is accentuated by the highly architectural shapes of hollies (*Ilex*) and perfectly pruned boxwood.

The view from the upper terrace is spectacular: the panorama includes the Arc de Triomphe, the Arche de La Défense and the surrounding skyscrapers, Montmartre and Sacré-Cœur, the Eiffel Tower, and the Montparnasse tower.

A terrace by Charlotte Perriand

This well-designed terrace is extremely simple. It surrounds the apartment entirely, offering a spectacular view all the way around. Charlotte Perriand, who designed this stylish garden, wanted to create an uncluttered space, without too many plants. She was also able to make use of the many chimney pots on top of the roof.

Charlotte Perriand planted a thicket of bamboo, which she likes for its suppleness and the poetic rustling of its leaves in the wind. The bare branches of the potted hazelnut tree and a corkscrew willow seem almost sculptural in the winter. Roses and wisteria add sophisticated touches of color to the overall scheme. The metal guardrail enclosing the terrace stops at waist level, so that it does not interfere with the view. When the large windows of the apartment are open, you feel as if you are sailing in space.

Below: Chimneystacks on the rooftop stand out against the magnificent late-afternoon sky.

Opposite: Light creates interesting effects in the contemporary apartment.

A sculptor's terrace

Above: Small square tiles encircle this thicket of bamboo. Phyllostachis aurea, which looks like a fountain.

Opposite: Yves de La Tour d'Auvergne's terrace is characterized by contrasts: white walls and floor tiles with the black of the ironwork. Rosemary grows in the raised bed, while sculptures by the artist have been placed on the ground.

Sculptor Yves de La Tour d'Auvergne lives in a former factory that he renovated. The artist's studios surround a patio, which lets sunlight enter and spread evenly through the space. This terrace gave Yves de La Tour d'Auvergne the idea of using a Mediterranean style for his house, characterized by simplicity and a white color scheme.

The patio was transformed into a terrace garden tiled in faience which is as white as the walls. The tiles encircle a bed planted with thyme, sage, rosemary, and even a few melons, hidden in a corner. The bedrooms and living areas all open onto the terrace. Works by the sculptor are placed all around the terrace; they look like mobiles moving in the wind and are placed on the ground as nonchalantly as if they were chaise longues.

A Virginia creeper softens the rather severe white walls and façade, but Yves de La Tour d'Auvergne makes a point of trimming it back; if he didn't, it would cut down the light and alter the deliberately austere style of the terrace. The contrast between white and black, walls and ironwork, gives a sculptural dimension to the space.

Even the plants here are used for their sculptural qualities, because the artist believes that nature must be "constrained" and controlled in its setting, much like the work of Japanese landscape artists in their minimalist gardens. A clump of *acuminata* bamboo, with thin spear-shaped foliage, creates an impression of fine rain when the wind blows through the leaves. The base is encircled by square tiles. The flowerbed, also surrounded by tiles, is thus surprisingly expressive, as is another bed, which is imprisoned in a glass cage like a fragile plant protected by a bell-glass.

Wood flooring and boxwood

Auguste Perret designed this house, meant to be a studio for artist Dora Gordine, in 1929. Its façade looks like a painting by Mondrian, and the garden in front of the house was created by A. Chemetoff. The façade is not a traditional wall, but an imaginative succession of offset panels, which form an irregular wall that gives the garden more space. The large chestnut tree, planted by Perret to filter the strong sunlight streaming into the studio, is still standing.

The terrace overlooks this garden as well as the others surrounding it. The lovely weathered wood flooring extends from the bedrooms. A white canvas cloth, modeled after those used on ocean liners, conceals the guardrail. Wooden frames that are exactly the same size as the skylights in the terrace, were laid out with boxwood pruned in alternating horizontal and vertical lines.

Below: A unique vegetable decoration: simple lines of boxwood planted in wooden boxes.

Opposite: The terrace design is in keeping with the style of the house, created in the late 1920s by Auguste Perret. Wooden frames placed on the old wooden flooring are planted with boxwood in alternating lines; the geometric patterns frame the skylights.

Pergolas and trellis

For the owners of this apartment, the decisive factors in their decision to move into this building were the large spaces inside and the immense terrace outside. At first this was an empty space, stuck between the chimneys of the neighboring buildings. It now has a small living room and a dining room with sliding glass doors that lead to an open area filled with plants.

Designed by the landscape architect Christiane Rivault, this terrace owes its charm and beauty to the division of the space into a series of open "rooms" and to the diversity of the materials used. The ground is covered with slabs of granite or wood, depending on the area; this alternating use of materials with different textures makes the terrace seem larger, while structuring the space. Various constructions include a veranda, a pergola, or paths between the chimneys, offering clear views and half-enclosed spaces that create a sense of depth, like a secret garden within the garden.

Christiane Rivault combines her talents as a landscape designer with her extensive botanical expertise to associate plants and colors. "She also understands very quickly what works with the personality of her clients," says the owner, "and, a very valuable asset, she likes to keep track of the gardens she has designed over a number of years." She planted a red camellia, a beautiful olive tree with silvery leaves, and a climbing jasmine, *Tracheolospermun jasminoides,* on the terrace next to the bathroom. The jasmine has fragrant white flowers in June.

The many plants on the terrace share the space with contemporary sculptures. In addition to the *sasanqua* camellias that bloom from November to February, there is also a lovely collection of ornamental grasses, which add a note of ethereal grace. These include *Carex pendula,* an elegant clump of shiny leaves from

Above: A cluster of clematis adds a graceful touch.

Opposite: A narrow passageway, lined with a mugo pine (Pinus mugo) and a Scots pine (Pinus sylvestris), which grow in containers along the edge of the veranda.

Following double page: The panoramic view from the veranda includes La Défense. Eglantine roses grow in the raised bed.

An outdoor living area has been set up on the wooden floor under the pergola; it is decorated with lovely oriental pottery. In the foreground to the left is a maple; in the background, birch trees and privet.

which emerge long stalks of hanging greenish-brown flowers; *Stipa tenuiflora,* with slender leaves that move in the slightest breeze; and *Miscanthus sinensis,* with surprising yellow- and green-striped leaves. Wild eglantine roses grow alongside *Solanum jasminoides,* a spectacular climber with clusters of small blue-violet flowers that bloom for six months of the year (June to November). A few trees, including maples and birches, provide some height, while heather grows around their trunks.

A mosaic on one of the sliding windows in the dining room seems to be floating in the air, as if in a

state of levitation. Made in Carthage, it is an enlarged copy of a mosaic, now in a museum there, with a ying-yang motif. The soft shades of the mosaic are perfectly balanced by the mottled violet and verdigris granite slabs and the grayish-white of the wooden flooring. The clean and sober lines of the garden furniture are very oriental in style. The small pieces of pottery are Japanese; the large ones, Chinese. There is an entire world of subtle nuances between the mosaic and the Chinese pottery, like the interplay of several overlapping cultures, a composition that links distant worlds.

The dining room has a granite floor. A large mosaic hangs on a glass panel separating the dining room from the garden section of the terrace. It is a copy of an ancient mosaic in the Carthage Museum. In the foreground to the right: the white flowers of Solanum jasminoides.

Index

The authors would like to thank all those who opened their doors to them, as well as the landscape gardeners and everyone else who made the book possible. Special thanks is given to Robert Bazelaire.